Pumpkins

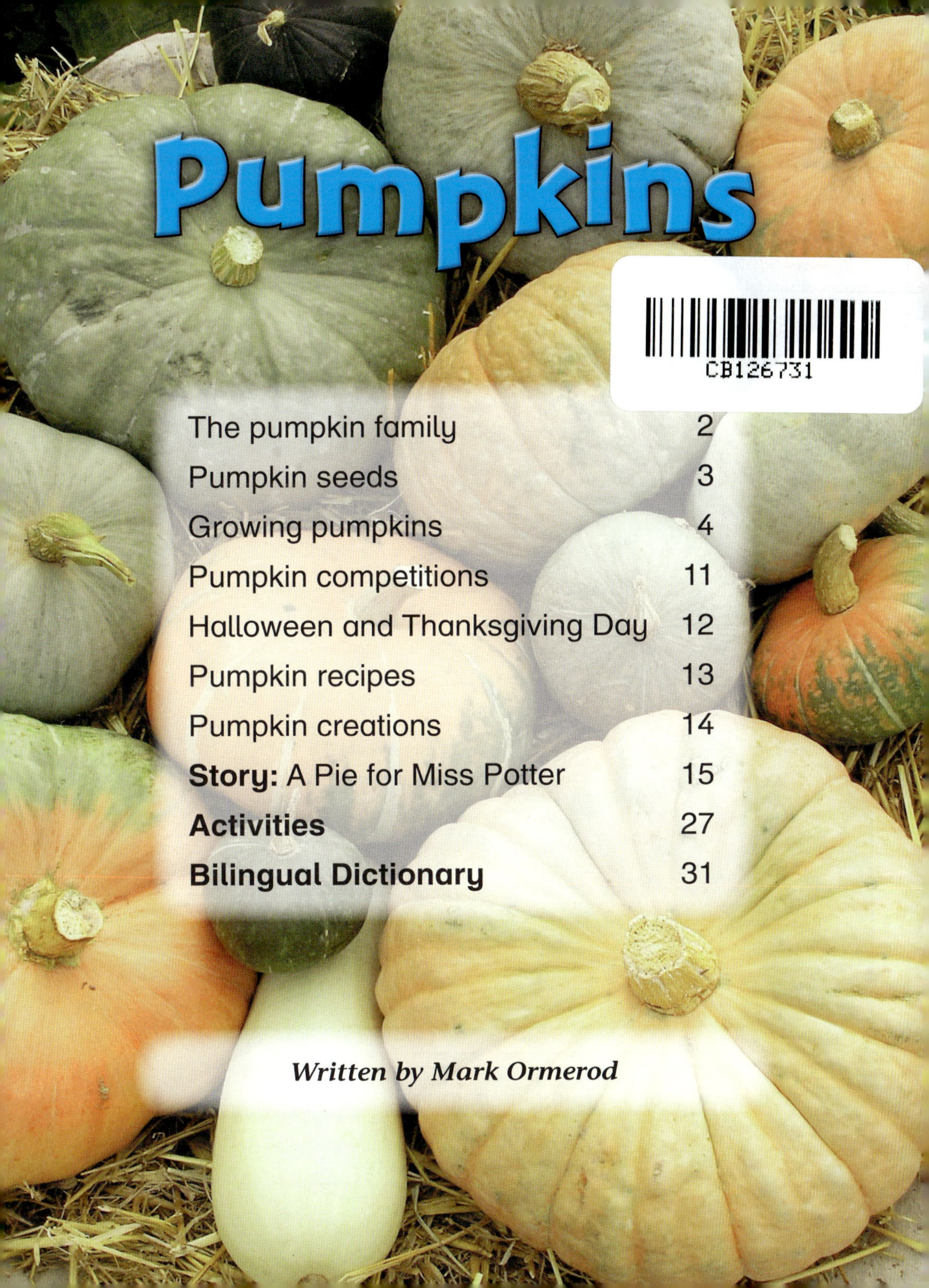

Written by Mark Ormerod

The pumpkin family

There are lots of different types of pumpkin. There are big pumpkins and small pumpkins. They are not all orange. There are also green, grey, yellow, brown and red pumpkins. Some pumpkins have got stripes.

Did you know that the pumpkin belongs to the same family of plants as the melon, the cucumber, the aubergine and the courgette?

Pumpkin seeds

These seeds are from a pumpkin. You can eat them. They are delicious and they've got a lot of vitamins.

You can also plant the seeds to grow more pumpkins.

Growing pumpkins

The best time to plant a pumpkin seed is at the end of spring. Plant it in a small pot or a plastic cup. Water it and keep it warm.

Seven to ten days after planting, the roots begin to grow. Then the stem begins to grow.

Three to four weeks after planting, the plant, which is called **a vine**, is a little bigger. The leaves are growing. You can now plant the vine outside.

The roots absorb water and food from the soil.

Snails love eating pumpkin leaves, so it's a good idea to protect the vine with a jar.

About six weeks after planting, the vine is much bigger. It has got more leaves.

Pumpkin vines grow very quickly in the sun. They grow along the ground and need a lot of space. A pumpkin stem can grow up to two metres long.

About ten weeks after planting, big yellow flowers appear on the vine. These flowers are not all the same. Some are male flowers and some are female flowers.

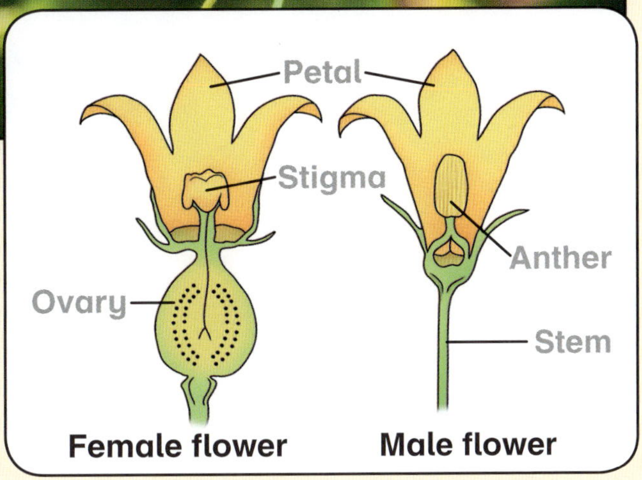

When a bee goes into a male flower to drink nectar, it gets covered with pollen. Then, when the bee goes into a female flower, pollen from the male flower sticks to the female flower. This is called **pollination**. After pollination, the plant can grow a pumpkin.

One day after pollination, the female flower dies and a pumpkin begins to grow.

About three weeks after pollination, the pumpkin is small and green.

About six weeks after pollination, the pumpkin is bigger and starts to turn orange.

About twelve weeks after pollination, the pumpkin is big and orange. It's ready to harvest.

Pumpkin competitions

Some towns in the USA have pumpkin competitions in the autumn. This giant pumpkin is the winner. It weighs an incredible 306 kilograms.

Giant pumpkins can weigh more than 750 kilograms – that's heavier than a cow.

Halloween and Thanksgiving Day

On the 31st October, many people in the USA make Jack-O-Lanterns from pumpkins to celebrate Halloween. At night, they put the lanterns in a window or in their gardens.

Many Americans make pumpkin pie to celebrate Thanksgiving Day, on the fourth Thursday of November.

Pumpkin recipes

Pumpkin pie isn't the only dish people make with pumpkins. Pumpkin bread and pumpkin cake are also very popular. Pumpkin soup is very easy to make. Why not make it at Halloween and serve it to your friends in a pumpkin bowl?

Pumpkin Soup

INGREDIENTS

- 12g of butter
- 1 onion, peeled and chopped
- 500g of pumpkin, peeled and chopped
- 1 tin of chopped tomatoes
- 750ml of chicken or vegetable stock
- salt and pepper

PREPARATION

Gently fry the onion in the butter until it is transparent.
Add the stock, tomatoes and the chopped pumpkin.
Boil for 20 minutes.
Liquidize the ingredients.
Add a pinch of salt and pepper.
Heat and serve.

Pumpkin creations

If you don't want to make a pie or a soup with your pumpkin, there are many other things you can make. Look at these original pumpkin creations for some ideas. You can make a pumpkin sculpture or a scarecrow family with pumpkin heads, or even take a ride in a pumpkin boat.

But remember to keep some seeds for planting!

A Pie for Miss Potter

Written by Mark Ormerod
Illustrated by Martin Impey

The summer holiday is over. It's 5th September, the first day of the new school year at St George's Primary School in London.
Hello, Mr Pike.
ST. GEORGE'S PRIMARY SCHOOL
Good morning, Sophie.
Who's that?
I think she's a teacher.
Boys and girls, this is our new teaching assistant. Her name is Miss Potter. She's from the USA and she's going to be with us for one year. I want you to make her feel very welcome.

The children ask Miss Potter some questions.

Everybody likes Miss Potter. She's very popular.

She's kind.

She's helpful.

She's easy to talk to.

She has a great sense of humour.

But one day in November, after school, Eduardo notices that Miss Potter looks unhappy.
Is everything okay, Miss Potter?
Yes, thank you, Eduardo. I'm homesick. I miss my family and friends in San Francisco.
I understand. I'm from Ecuador. I sometimes miss my family and friends too.
Eduardo shows Miss Potter a photo of his grandparents. Then, Miss Potter shows Eduardo a photo of her family.
These are my parents. That's my older brother and my younger sister.

The next day, in the computer room, Eduardo talks to his friends Sophie, Tom, Alice and Lily.
Miss Potter is feeling homesick. What can we do?
How about a party?
Or a cake?
No, not a cake. Next Thursday is 25th November. It's Thanksgiving Day in the USA. We can make her a pumpkin pie.
THANKSGIVING DAY
That's a great idea, Sophie. Let's look for a recipe on the Internet.

After school, the children go to Sophie's house to make the pumpkin pie. They have all the ingredients they need: sugar, spices, eggs, flour, butter, milk and an enormous pumpkin.
That's a big pumpkin.
It's from my grandfather's garden.
Don't make a mess, children.

Tom reads the recipe. Sophie and Alice make the pastry. Eduardo and Lily peel the pumpkin.

Everybody helps to make the pumpkin mixture.
Whoops!
Sorry, Tom!
Oh, no!

While the pie is in the oven, the children clean the kitchen.
It looks good.

When Sophie's mother comes in, everything is clean and the pie is ready.
The pie looks delicious. Well done!

The next day, during the break, Lily asks Miss Potter to come to the classroom.
Is there a problem?
No, Miss Potter. There's something we want you to see. It's something nice.
In the classroom, all the children are waiting to surprise Miss Potter.

There are decorations on the wall. There's pumpkin pie for everyone. Miss Potter is very surprised and very happy.
Happy Thanksgiving Day.
We want to thank you for everything you do for us.

Here are some photos of San Francisco to make you feel at home.
This is incredible!

Miss Potter enjoys looking at all the photos of San Francisco.
That's the Golden Gate Bridge. It's so beautiful. I think it's my favourite place in the world.
Thank you, everybody. Thanksgiving Day is my favourite day of the year at home and I'm very happy to celebrate it in London with you all!
And now I'm going to have a slice of this very delicious pumpkin pie.

Activities

1 Write and label.

~~pumpkin~~ leaf flower seeds roots soil pot

2 Number the sentences in the correct order.

- [ ] The pumpkin gets bigger and begins to turn orange.
- [ ] After the flower dies, a pumpkin begins to grow.
- [1] You plant a seed.
- [ ] After pollination, the female flower dies.
- [ ] First the roots begin to grow.
- [ ] You see leaves growing on the stem.
- [ ] Bees pollinate the flowers.
- [ ] The pumpkin is ready to harvest.
- [ ] After the leaves, the flowers start to appear.
- [ ] Then the stem begins to grow.

3 Circle T (True) or F (False).

1 All pumpkins are orange. T (F)

2 The best time to plant a pumpkin seed is at the end of spring. T F

3 Snails love eating pumpkin soup. T F

4 A pumpkin stem can grow up to ten metres long. T F

5 All pumpkin flowers are the same. T F

6 Some towns in the USA have pumpkin competitions. T F

7 Halloween is on 31st August. T F

8 In the USA, Thanksgiving Day is in November. T F

4 Complete the crossword.

1 

2 

3 

4 

5 

6 

7 

8 

9 

10 

5 Complete the sentences.

clean	~~ask~~	shows	look for	thanks	make	asks	enjoys	peel

1 The children ___ask___ Miss Potter a lot of questions.

2 Miss Potter ____________ Eduardo a photo of her family.

3 The children ____________ a recipe on the Internet.

4 Sophie and Alice ____________ the pastry.

5 Eduardo and Lily ____________ the pumpkin.

6 The children ____________ the kitchen.

7 Lily ____________ Miss Potter to come to the classroom.

8 Miss Potter ____________ looking at the photos of San Francisco.

9 Miss Potter ____________ the children for her Thanksgiving Day surprise.

6 Write the questions for Miss Potter.

1 are / Where / from / in / the / you / USA?

Where are you from in the USA?

Miss Potter: I'm from San Francisco.

2 London? / Do / like / you

____

Miss Potter: Yes, I like London very much.

3 sport? / What's / favourite / your

____

Miss Potter: I haven't got a favourite sport.

4 Do / any / play / instruments? / you

____

Miss Potter: Yes, I do. I play the guitar.

5 speak? / you / languages / do / What

____

Miss Potter: I speak English and Spanish.

7 Who said what? Match the speech bubbles to the pictures.

1 It's from my grandfather's garden.

2 The pie looks delicious. Well done!

3 I want you to make her feel very welcome.

4 Thanksgiving Day is my favourite day of the year.

5 I sometimes miss my family and friends, too.

6 We want to thank you for everything you do for us.

8 Write the missing vowels *a*, *e*, *i*, *o* or *u*.

1 Miss Potter is very p o p u l a r.

2 She's k _ n d.

3 She's h _ l p f _ l.

4 She's _ _ sy to talk to.

5 She's got a great s _ n s_ _f h _ m _ _ r

Bilingual Dictionary

Key: (n) = noun (v) = verb (adj) = adjective

Write the words in your language.

add (v) ______
appear (v) ______
autumn (n) ______
bee (n) ______
begin (v) ______
bridge (n) ______
butter (n) ______
chop (v) ______
clean (v) ______
competition (n) ______
delicious (adj) ______
eggs (n) ______
enormous (adj) ______
feel (v) ______
female (adj) ______
giant (adj) ______
great (adj) ______
grow (v) ______
Halloween (n) ______
harvest (v) ______
helpful (adj) ______
ingredients (n) ______
keep (v) ______
kind (adj) ______
kitchen (n) ______
lantern (n) ______
leaves (n) ______
male (adj) ______
melon (n) ______
miss (v) ______
mixture (n) ______
nectar (n) ______
notice (v) ______
older (adj) ______
oven (n) ______
pastry (n) ______
peel (v) ______
photo (n) ______
pie (n) ______
place (n) ______
plant (v) ______
pollination (n) ______
pot (n) ______
pumpkin (n) ______
recipe (n) ______
roots (n) ______
scarecrow (n) ______
seeds (n) ______
show (v) ______
slice (n) ______
spices (n) ______
spring (n) ______
start (v) ______
stem (n) ______
stick (v) ______
stripes (n) ______
vitamins (n) ______
warm (adj) ______
water (v) ______
weigh (v) ______
welcome (adj) ______
younger (adj) ______

Macmillan Education
4 Crinan Street
London N1 9XW
A division of Springer Nature Limited
Companies and representatives throughout the world

ISBN 978-1-3800-3843-2

First published 2012
This edition published 2019

Designed by Carolyn Gibson
Illustrated by Martin Impey and Mark Turner
Photo research by Emily Taylor

The author and publishers would like to thank the following for permission to reproduce their images: **Alamy**/ Alamy Celebrity p14(tl), Alamy/ Alaska Stock p11(m), Alamy/ Bon Appetit p13(t), Alamy/ Anne Gilbert p6, Alamy/ Dave Halley p10(tr), Alamy/ Simon Reddy p12(b), Alamy Stock Photo/mauritius images GmbH p9(bl), Alamy/ inga Spence p9; Corbis/ Creativ Studio Heinemann/Westend61 p3(m); **Getty Images/Digital Vision/ Jamie Garbutt** p12(t), Getty Images/E+/tacojim p14(tr), Getty Images/EyeEm/Slobodan Kovacevic p3(seeds), Getty Images/ Minden Pictures p8, Getty Images/Westend61 p7; **Photolibrary** p10(m), Photolibrary/ Emilio Ereza p1, **Rex Features**/ Norman Betts p14(b).

Cover photography courtesy of Getty Images/ Tim Kitchen

Printed and bound in Great Britain by Bell and Bain Ltd, Glasgow

2023 2022 2021 2020 2019
10 9 8 7 6 5 4 3 2 1